Coming Out Of
THE WOODS

MARLENE ESSENCE DOTTS

CITI OF
BOOKS

CITIOFBOOKS, INC.

3736 Eubank NE Suite A1

Albuquerque, NM 87111-3579

www.citiofbooks.com

Hotline: 1 (877) 389-2759

Fax: 1 (505) 930-7244

Ordering Information:

Quantity sales. Special discounts are available on quantity purchases by corporations, associations, and others. For details, contact the publisher at the address above.

Printed in the United States of America.

ISBN-13:   Softcover   979-8-89391-289-0

              Ebook   979-8-89391-290-6

Library of Congress Control Number: 2024917362

The time has come for me to come out of the woods. So many times, I felt like I had no life to live.

"Do you ever feel or felt like life was not worth living?"

"Why?"

I broke these chains that kept me bound, that had me in self-captivity. I was in my prison without prison bars. As I discovered in rehab, I was faced with many challenges that had been going on with me that I had yet to confront. As I look back on my life, I should be dead more than alive. I've been dead spiritually, emotionally, as well as mentally—mentally broken.

When I started writing, different faces emerged. I had so many faces but yet didn't know which one was me. The real me, Marlene, is still getting to know herself, but she is getting so much better at it. Just accepting to take one day at a time and asking for guidance from her higher power, instead of relying on her own understanding to make bad decisions or choices.

Taking the time to glance back, but not to stare, is important in order to move forward. Moving forward to see what's ahead is more positive than staring backward. Backward is deceiving, lying—drugs and alcohol, the devil's playgrounds. We consider all these things fun until it isn't anymore.

Focusing on other people, gossiping in negative ways, and being negative. Not being happy with yourself, suffering in your own guilt or someone else's pain.

I'm also learning to live the 12 steps. You don't have to be an addict to use these 12 steps of N.A. or A.A. I mentioned in my previous book that different faces—we're all addicted to something. Even sex!

Sometimes I can't help but wonder what type of person I would have been if I hadn't been raised by the parents I had.

"Who knows?"

My therapist asked me, and I still wonder: "Would I have been better or worse? Maybe I could've been with a good family." I wonder, was it meant for me to be me?

So I can tell this story and maybe help to save someone else's life. Giving a little light of hope to cling to! I'm hoping when I'm done, I can touch someone. Help somebody like somebody helped me since I last wrote Different Faces.

I have had so many life challenges. I remember before leaving rehab, I was thinking about how I fought and how I accomplished getting into the halfway house. I went to culinary school and finished with a certificate of completion, completed halfway, and now I'm in my very own apartment—it hasn't been easy. It was a struggle, but yet I did not consider using a drug. Sometimes we don't know our strengths until the struggles are forced upon us. If I fought to get this far, I can continue to fight for my life.

I remember being in the halfway house when I was going to school and didn't have any money. I couldn't find a job; every interview I went to was promising. I went back to the halfway house so excited, telling everyone I got the position as a cook. The jobs I went to, the manager told me that I had the job, but on two occasions, when I called to see when I could start, the hiring manager told me they hired someone more suitable for the position. I was hurt! Feelings of discouragement came over me. All I knew was that I had to keep going forward no matter what. It wasn't me; it was something much greater than me.

I had a bus ticket—a 1-zone. It took a 3-zone bus ticket to get me to school, from Paterson, NJ, to Bloomfield, NJ. I'm walking down the street to the bus terminal with tears flowing down my face. I tried to stop the tears from flowing, trying not to let anyone see me crying. The tears just wouldn't stop. Finally, I got halfway to the bus stop.

As I'm wiping the tears from my face, I'm thinking, I can't do this! At that moment, I wanted to go back home and do what I was used to doing—and that was selling drugs, using drugs, and alcohol. Another part of me said, "That's not an option." I sucked up my pride and my tears. I got on the bus and whispered to the bus driver, "I have no money." I was embarrassed, trying not to let the riders hear me. The bus driver let me on the bus. It was such a relief, thinking... just for today, I have a way home. Not worried about tomorrow or what tomorrow may bring.

Some days, some of the bus drivers would ride past me because they knew I had no money. I'm on the bus, looking at everyone on the bus, wondering what their life is like. Wondering, are they struggling? Are they happy? What are they going through? Even in the mornings, going to school, I would see homeless people sleeping on the streets. It saddened me to see these people, thinking that I once was like them— "homeless," with no one to turn to!

I'm starting to see the miracle of God's work. I'm not homeless anymore. I walk in the door of the halfway house, and one of the staff members came to me and said, "If you need money to get back and forth to school, I can help you!"

This lady knows nothing about me for her to come to me and say that. But I didn't know how to accept the offer because where I come from, people always want something in return. Until I thought about, "How would I get back and forth to school?" I accepted the offer. My husband, Chris, sent me money whenever he could. We were no longer together but ended up being the best of friends.

I did promise to pay her back. She said, "Marlene, you don't have to! I see that you're trying. I see your motivation. I see when you get up and go to school every morning, even when you're sick."

I'm thinking to myself, just an hour ago, I was thinking of giving up! Before moving into my apartment, I went through some struggles. Monmouth County sent my voucher to Newark; I found an apartment in East Orange. Newark sent my voucher back to Monmouth County, and then Monmouth County had to send it to East Orange.

Months passed, and I was about to lose my Section 8 voucher. The landlord held my apartment for me for two months while I tried to get the security deposit. He still waited. He could've given it to anyone else, but he didn't. All these recurring events I think about when I feel like giving up.

There is hope—you just have to believe. Things may seem bad, but just remember, it doesn't last forever. I get aggravated, impatient, and want things to go my way. I take a moment to breathe, think about someone who could be going through more difficult times than I am, and remind myself, just don't give up!

Moving into my apartment, I had a bed and a TV my daughter, Tiarrah, had given me. The TV was small, and I could only get channels 11, 7, and 2. The only way I could watch TV was to put an antenna on the back of it and position the TV until the picture was clear. But I was grateful!

I'm involved in a program called the ISP. I stayed involved and connected when I went on a retreat in Mendham, NJ. The ISP reaches out to halfway houses to recruit men and women who are in recovery or trying to recover by bringing them to the retreat to get a spiritual connection to their higher power. They have a guest speaker called "The Witness," who comes on this weekend retreat to tell their story of addiction.

Everyone has their own story of addiction—some are the same, some are different. In the end, we are all the same, fighting for the greater good in ourselves, our lives, and selfhealing! After hearing that these ladies recruited us, I wondered what they knew about addiction if they had never used a drug or been addicted to alcohol. I wondered how they understood it, as all they knew was what they read from a book.

I'd rather go to a counselor who's been where I've been. People look at you differently when they don't understand addiction. I realized after the retreat that they were faced with different addictions other than alcohol or drugs. That thing called "life on life's terms"—that I talked about in Different Faces—came to reality. We don't ever see the other part of addiction that people face, like being enablers to our kids or our spouse. It's sometimes hard to accept addiction until it hits your home. So now, what do we do about it?

No book teaches you not to pick up a drug or drink alcohol before you pick up for the first time. You may hear from other people how drugs are bad, and so now we want to know how bad they are. We want to try them, thinking we can handle them, even though we see how people act or look when using drugs and alcohol. But do you know what we say?

IT WON'T HAPPEN TO ME.

We're not invisible! No book teaches you to live life on life's terms!

So you think! There is one book out here, and that book is the Bible. In the Bible, some scriptures teach us how to live. We find it hard to live by these rules; they're too difficult. We want to live life the way we see fit to our lives. That makes us learn along the way— that's learning the hard way. Like the old saying, Once you've made your bed, now you have to lie in it.

Meeting these women was a great learning experience. Christy reached out to all the women who attended the retreat to have a reunion. I attended along with other women who came, and most of us completed the halfway house.

Christy asked if I needed anything. I replied, "Yes, because I had nothing." All I knew was that everyone started donating—donations were coming from everyone. No one has ever treated me the way these ladies have. They knew me from nowhere but from the halfway house.

Now, I have a bigger TV, dishes, a bathroom set, a kitchen table, and furniture. It felt so good to have gotten my keys in my hand. When I put the key in the door and turned the knob, a relief came over me, thinking how hard I fought to get to this point in my life. And now, I have such amazing people in my life.

Susan and her husband came to my apartment. They put blinds and curtains up, helped me clean the apartment. I remember them saying,

"We have to make sure you have curtains. We don't want anybody looking in your windows." I thought to myself, Wow, these people care about me. How could I possibly turn back to my old ways and behaviors? I knew I couldn't.

Have you ever had someone who knew you from nowhere and did all this for you, went out of their way to help you? No, not me! People always wanted something in return. I'm forever grateful!

The first night in my apartment, I sat in silence, tears of joy, thanking God. This feeling was so different from the first time I got my very first apartment. This apartment—I was grateful for it. The gratitude of losing everything reminded me of not taking things or life for granted.

I knew that my brothers were in jail for robbing the neighbor that resided next door to them and my mom, but to see it on TV that they both were being given 15–20 years if found guilty, I said to myself, Oh, shit, they made headlines this time! I haven't followed the story; a part of me didn't care, until I was asked to come to their sentencing by Stacey. She said that their lawyers said it would be nice if some family members showed up on their behalf.

But before their sentencing, I told her no. At first, I didn't want to be or get involved with anyone. I still had resentment issues; I didn't want to help or see anyone's face again—not even my mother. I was at the point that if she died, I would be okay with it. I was still angry at the fact that, no matter what my mom has ever done to me in my life, I was still always the one there for her.

I remember when my brother Jerome punched me in the face and broke my ankle. She didn't even call to check on me. She said I was lying and stopped talking to me, then had the nerve to come to my house arguing about a crockpot that she let me borrow. I was on crutches, my lips were swollen, one of my teeth was loose from the impact of the punch, but she never asked, Marlene, are you okay?

I'm telling Stacey why I don't want to get involved. Stacey was shocked at what I was telling her; she understood where I was coming from. I said it has always been that way— everything they have ever done wrong, my mom was always blind to it. She just wouldn't accept the ignorance they both endured. She would always take their side. I remember getting beatings and being punished for their actions growing up.

Stacey was my brother Jermaine's girlfriend. As we were talking, I didn't really want to talk to her, but I listened. She started to tell me the story of everything that was happening. I got the story of the night that it happened—my daughter Lateria's boyfriend, Carlos, hit and robbed the guy.

My twin brother knew the guy. He lived next door to my mom and he was a veteran. Days before the sentencing, I called my brother's lawyer to find out what was going on, but it was too late for anything at this point.

All my brother did was know the guy, and they planned to rob him. But did they actually do it? No. But all the times they've been in jail for drugs and assaults—not just me, but other women they beat on—and my mom always thought it was okay for them to beat on women. Out of all people, she should have known what it felt like to have a man pounding and kicking on her.

My mom was also an alcoholic, and our father died of AIDS—he was an intravenous heroin addict. This is the part when life catches up with you. The disease of addiction entered my family and destroyed a lot of us.

The public defenders didn't even care. I called to speak with Jermaine's lawyer. He had an attitude, like, It's too late at this point. The trial was over months ago. I'm thinking, my brothers got railroaded. My brothers were heroin and crack users. Carlos was an alcoholic bully who sold drugs in the area. He said he didn't know the guy, and I know that was a lie.

Did I care? For some reason, I did. I started getting involved. The day before the sentencing, Stacey came to my apartment early the next morning. Now I'm living in East Orange, NJ. Stacey lived in Maryland. She picked me up, then we had to go pick up my mom. She lived in Neptune, NJ with my cousin Linda.

My brothers and I never really got along, and I can thank my mom for that. Just that moment, just thinking how it could've been me—all over drugs. I've never robbed anyone for drugs or anything for that matter. I sold my body, I stole out of stores, but to have been with the wrong people or back and forth to jail for drugs, which I have been, would've gotten me some years. But I thank God that He saw something in me that I didn't see in myself.

In silence, as we had already picked up my mother, we are riding to Freehold, NJ, to the courthouse to see my brothers, my mother's sons, get sentenced. The officers brought them in individually. Jermaine came in first, as the judge read off the charges and sentenced him to 15 years, and then Jerome, my other brother. I had an outburst in the courtroom. The judge ordered the officer to escort me out of the courtroom.

When the court was over, I spoke to Jermaine's lawyer, and I said, "You could have seen the criminal background and seen that my brothers had drug issues. They need help. How many times have they been to jail for drugs and no one has ever offered them both rehab? Jail doesn't help! They need rehab!"

Carlos gets 1-year probation. I couldn't believe it. After dropping my mom off, Stacey and I came back to my house and were looking over the paperwork to see if there was anything we could find. We found that the victim said that Jerome and Jermaine didn't hit him. He told the detectives that, and that wasn't brought up in court during the trial.

I had a chance to speak to the victim. He was fierce. Hearing that Carlos got 1-year probation, I also knew him. He was a nice guy, and he didn't deserve to have gotten beaten in his apartment. My brothers were in the apartment. Jermaine went to go ask him to help with some paperwork. Until my mother called them, they went to go see what my mom wanted. By the time they were walking back to the victim's apartment, Carlos was coming out of the victim's apartment. He pointed out Carlos as the one who attacked him in his apartment.

I knew I needed more therapy, so I sought my therapist since I'd been out of the halfway house. I discussed this issue with the therapist, and I was advised not to get involved. I still had issues that I had to fix within myself. I had to work on myself. But did I listen? No. I continued to call lawyers to help, to see if we could all chip in to help my brothers with getting an appeal.

As days went on, I had to start putting me first. I had to remember that in NA, we have to be selfish. It's a selfish program. I started getting so wrapped up that I was forgetting about myself again. So, I had to explain to Stacey that I can't right now. I have to focus on myself. And she understood where I was coming from.

See, I acknowledged that I was losing focus on myself during that time. I kept praying and praying to ask God, "What should I do?" Every day I kept thinking less and less about my brothers' issues. It's not that I didn't care, but I had to put me first. What I learned in the ISP program was how to let go of baggage. Baggage can become so heavy that, eventually, it becomes too much to carry. I refused to carry baggage or anyone's garbage anymore!

Then I started realizing there was nothing more I could do. For example, when you die, you can't take anything with you. You leave behind your house, family, etc... All you take is you... yourself! Some people want to take stuff with them, but you can't. Sometimes, taking yourself is better than taking others or taking on other people's stuff. You have to leave things behind. Imagine if you had to carry your house or car, even family members, with you! Believe me, before you get to where you're going, you'll drop it all off. You'll look back and say, "I'll be back for you!" Not to be selfish, but how do you take care of others when you can't even take care of yourself?

I sent Stacey some pages out of my NA book to share with my brothers when I was able to talk with them in three-way calls. I gave them words of encouragement. I told them to take the time to do some thinking and self-reflection on themselves. I told them to get help while in prison. "God put you guys there for a reason. You're not dead. You all have a chance to get it right. You guys are alive." They had a good life, better than I did. I didn't. They were able to play sports and enjoy their childhood. I wasn't allowed to enjoy mine.

I had to rush home from school, cook dinner, help them with their homework, clean the house, and have them in bed before my mom got home from work. I became a maid, a slave, a nanny, and a mom. I remember my mom beating me because my brothers started calling me "mommy." They were 1, and I was 9 years old. I was able to tell them apart when no one else could. When my parents didn't want to get up with them in the middle of the night, I did, but I got blamed for them calling me mommy.

If I was late picking them up from my grandparents, I would be in trouble. My grandparents lived next door to us. They were my father's parents. I couldn't even go on field trips. I was robbed of everything— even my virginity. As my brothers and I talked, I told them, "Y'all had the best of everything." My parents didn't buy me Nikes or up-to-date clothes and shoes. They would dress me in hand-me-down clothes, and I was teased in school. They got the football and wrestling trophies, so I guess it doesn't matter what type of parents I had or if I was rich or poor. This addiction comes into every family. I told them, "Whatever is the God of your understanding, seek Him now! You're going to need Him." I don't know if they listened. They both had a lot to think about. They both had three years in jail already.

Days later, Susan calls and says, "Marlene, I'm on my way." Her husband and his friend pulled up with a U-Haul, and then she arrived. Moments later, telling me to meet her outside, I was able to let them in my apartment. I helped bring stuff in, but I had to go to work. When I got home from work, my apartment was breathtaking. They color-coordinated every room. It was so homey and beautiful. All I could say was, "Wow!" I slowly walked to the bedroom, then to the bathroom. I thought to myself, "This is so unbelievable." I couldn't believe how people are placed in our lives—people who asked for nothing in return.

The next day, I called Susan and thanked her. I just couldn't thank her enough. Thinking back to when I went to the halfway house, my intention wasn't to stay there. I knew that once I got out of rehab... well, as I thought, I was getting out of the halfway house and getting my Section 8 back. It was so easy in my mind. See, God had a way of showing me His way. See, when you ask God for guidance and help, you have to be willing to receive what you're asking for, so you have to be careful what or how you ask. He knew I wasn't ready. I was still sick mentally. There was something else God needed me to see... witness.

After pleading and fighting to get into this halfway house and having Mr. Derwin put his neck on the line to get me here, when I got to the halfway house, I called my worker to inform her that I was now in the halfway house. She congratulated me on completing the rehab and how she was rooting for me. That was strange coming from her. Then she goes on to tell me that when I finish the halfway house, she had my voucher waiting for me. My heart dropped with no understanding. I was thinking to myself, while on the phone, "What the f***..." Then I called Chris, apologizing for the way I treated him while he was in the hospital. I realized that two wrongs don't make a right.

After hanging up with Chris, I asked one of the ladies who was residing at the halfway house, "How long is this program?" She said, "4-6 months." I said, "4-6 months!" I figured I would talk to the counselor to inform her that I no longer needed to be there. After my worker had just told me I had to complete the halfway house, it's so funny now!

The first day at the halfway house, my bunkie, Tina, was there. She left the rehab a few days before I did. She was upset about going to the halfway house, but she had to go. She was on drug court, and this halfway house was for drug court clients. I was told that I may not be there for long. I was there because I was an SAI client. I wasn't mandated, but I was homeless, so I didn't know whether to unpack my belongings or what.

Tina showed me around the house. Rose was there—she was one of the ladies I didn't get along with. We bumped heads a few times in the rehab, and she was one of the ladies I gave a hug on the way out the door as she was leaving. Tina was telling me how hungry she was, and I looked surprised and shocked. I asked, "Why don't they feed you here?" Her reply was, "Yeah, only dinner." I looked at her and said,

"Only dinner! So how are we supposed to eat?" She said she hadn't gotten her food stamps yet.

I asked her, "Do they have a pantry?" She said, "Yeah." I said to her, "Show me." As we walked toward the kitchen, one of the ladies was in the TV room, and I asked, "Can I cook something to eat?" I knew at some point this place was better than the rehab. I introduced myself, and she said, "Hi, my name is Sharon." Sharon took me into the pantry, letting me take items out to cook. I said to Tina, "You can cook for yourself, there's food here!" Tina said to me, "Marlene, I can't cook." I laughed.

I said to Tina, "I got you, I'll cook something for you." Sharon came in the kitchen and said, "You can cook!" I replied, "Can I?" I was laughing. It was almost dinner, so I whipped up something really quick. I got the Oodles of Noodles, went in the fridge, got peppers and onions, sautéed the onions and peppers, and added tuna. I boiled the noodles until almost done, then stir-fried everything until it was finished.

Tina was so happy. She said, "When I get my food stamps, I want you to cook for me all the time!" Sharon immediately took me under her wing, explaining to me, "Don't get stuck in the kitchen because you won't have a life. Everyone will want you to cook all the time." I said to Sharon, "But I don't mind." Sharon looked at me and said, "I'm telling you, Marlene, you will regret it." Sharon went on explaining to me about the do's and don'ts.

As the evening went on, I still hadn't unpacked my belongings. Then I was called into the office, and I was told to go to room 7. I said to Tina, "We're bunkies again!" I couldn't take a top bunk because of my back injury, so I was given a single bed. Newcomers have a 30-day blackout where we couldn't go anywhere by ourselves.

At dinner, the staff ordered food and offered me some Chinese food. It was so good. I only took a little, not trying to be greedy—it was chicken wings, ribs, and fried rice. 42 days in rehab of not having outside food felt like I was there longer than 42 days. It was the best thing ever. The staff insisted for me to take more, and I couldn't resist, so I did.

Then I saw that I could have my cell phone. I called my daughter Tiarrah and told her to bring me my cell phone. I had to give it to Ashley upon checking into the rehab. I was thinking to myself, "This is awesome, not bad after all." We could go outside and smoke a cigarette without being escorted. We were able to go out all day except during meeting times, cleaning, and dinner. This way worked so much better for me.

Even though being on a 30-day blackout and not able to go anywhere without an escort, one of the ladies was going to the store. Tina and I went along with her. It felt so good to get out of the house. I wasn't used to walking. We had to walk everywhere, except if we had to go to court or welfare, we would get escorted by a member of the house who had been at the halfway house. We had to walk to meetings in groups 3-4 times a week. I hated it!

After a week, I had one of my weekly sessions with the counselor of the halfway house and asked her, "How long do I have to be here?" She said, "At least 4 months." I told her that I had my voucher. She replied, "You still have to complete the program." I said to the staff member, "I can't be doing all this walking after coming back from an AA meeting." Her reply was, "You walked to get your drugs." I laughed and said, "No, I didn't. I had a car or it was delivered to me." We chuckled. They said, "Well, you will be walking!"

All the staff members were once addicts themselves. They were employed to work at the halfway house. You can see how some people forget where they came from to judge someone. I've learned to look at the inner soul of oneself to seek self-reservation before judgment. You just may never know the person you judged. The skeleton you're hiding could be much greater. But you'll never tell. The inside can be so cut and bruised, screaming for help, but on the outside, we learn to cover it all up—pain, the guilt, regrets, the untold stories that are dying to get unleashed. Learning to live one day at a time is hard, but it's getting easier every day.

I learned quickly how to stay out of the halfway house, so I wouldn't get involved with hesay, she-say shit, or get involved with other people's problems and addictions. It's easy to get caught up, and I wanted no parts of it. I started culinary school before my 30-day blackout was over. I started to learn how to navigate myself everywhere I needed to go, transforming from a small town that I came from to a city. I loved that there were buses that ran every 15 minutes and you could always catch a bus or the light rail. You could never be stuck or stranded.

I learned how to find meetings. I downloaded the bus app to know what bus to get on. I would leave the house at 6 a.m., and sometimes not return till 10 p.m. Not being in the house gave me clarity. It gave me time to spend with myself. Sometimes when I got home, the staff would check my pocketbook or bookbag. I didn't mind it or care. I was doing all the right things. I was determined.

I could tell that one of the staff members didn't like me but couldn't catch me. Every time I would come in the house, she would give me a look. I knew what that look meant, but I

didn't care. Even on certain days, I would meet up with other women at meetings that ended at 9–9:30 p.m., and we would all walk home together. Sometimes we would get a ride or take a Lyft home.

How I got involved with the ISP:

It was a month of being in the halfway house. The staff put a list out asking who wanted to go on a retreat. I'd never heard of a retreat. I thought it was a Gospel Fest, and that was something I wanted and felt like I needed to go. I asked one of the staff, "Can I go?" She said no at first. "You have to be 3 months sober to go," she said. I was coming up on two months, so a few days later, I asked again. She said, "Put your name on the list," so I did.

The time came, and I was so overjoyed to go, not knowing what to expect. All I knew was that I was out of the house for the weekend and going to a Gospel Fest. A week had passed, and I was looking forward to this festival. We were all going for the weekend, but still, I had no clue what I was looking forward to! Other women and I were all packed and ready to go. The ladies from the retreat came to escort us.

Cathy was short with blonde hair. Christy was tall, thin, and her smile was bright. It lit up the room.

Rebecca, she had dark hair, very nice woman. It was an hour ride—if it wasn't, it felt like it was. When we arrived, there were other women from other halfway houses, some women I knew and some I didn't know. It was breathtaking. The retreat was held at Saint Margaret Retreat House in Mendham, NJ. Across from there was where the nuns lived.

When we got inside, we were shown our rooms. We were each given our separate rooms. I hadn't slept in my own room since I got evicted from my apartment. After making our beds, we were all greeted downstairs. We put on our name tags, and they had snacks—fruit, coffee, and tea—out for the taking. In my mind, I'm saying to myself, When is the Gospel Fest going to happen? We were given pamphlets explaining the retreat house and the rules of the retreat. Then it went on to say about respecting each other—whatever we discuss, no one is to repeat.

ISP stands for Ignatian Spirituality Project. ISP exists to "light the path forward." Participants can begin to find the acceptance, hope, and healing needed to reclaim their lives. ISP approaches the tradition of 12 steps. Everyone needs to practice the 12 steps. It's a step and a walk toward everyday life. Also, the Serenity Prayer—through every situation in life, whether it's at work, school, or home—is to be used in every part of your life. You will start finding meaning in it. It will also humble your heart and mind. No matter how badly we want things to go our way, sometimes it can't. Then, we start finding new meaning to move forward positively.

You will find your life so much more meaningful. I know we're human, and we're going to worry and take things out of context at some point. Take a moment to stop and say the Serenity Prayer or read the 12 steps. You will see it. You will feel it. Then, you'll find a different approach to handling situations, and that's what the retreat is about.

The founders, the sponsors, ISP out of Chicago, who started this project, are awesome people who put this program together to stop homelessness. They want to take the time to help people like me and you! They don't look at you differently from them, and that is what makes the program awesome. See, in our minds, we tend to start judging people before we meet them, or we judge people by what others say about them. Or you're being judged by the way a person looks.

Before you judge anyone—LOOK AT YOURSELF! STOP! Placing a tag on another person, the ISP team has done so much for me that no one else has done in my life. I'm not talking about the stuff they've given me or helped me with, I'm talking about seeing the light—the light that can be bright only if you're willing to walk toward it. It was a women's retreat. It was also a men's retreat, but that was held at a different retreat house. This is how I stayed connected, and I'm moving up in rank, in training to be a witness, and hopefully someday I'll be traveling as an ambassador of hope, telling my stories to many women who are struggling with addiction.

They support me in every positive way. This retreat can turn your life around. It's just like everything else: you have to want it. At the end of the night, after we finished, Ann Brown, one of the witnesses who came from Chicago to tell her story, spoke to us. At the end of the evening, we all sat there. The spirit was really moving in that room. Even after we prayed, it was so comforting just being in that room with candles lit. No one wanted to get up. Once everyone got up, some women went out for a cigarette, and some went to their rooms.

I'm sitting in the kitchen, having tea before turning in for bed. Ann walks in, sits down next to me, holds my hand, and says, "Marlene, where are you going from here?" Tears are flowing down my cheeks, and I look at her and say, "I don't know." At that moment, that night, there was something way beyond me watching over me. Something way beyond me was there. There were many women there—why did she pick me to come to? I'd never met this lady before until that day. I'd only known her for four hours. They say we all have angels that guide us and direct us. We have to be willing to let them in.

The next day, we did the same thing: we laughed, we cried, we even hugged each other. It felt good to share our thoughts without judgment. After breakfast, and toward the end of the night, we all did arts and crafts while listening to music. We were given paper to write a letter to God.

On the last day of the retreat, we had breakfast and lunch before leaving. We all wrote a letter to God, writing as if we were sending the letter in the mail. Cathy said she would mail the letters out in a month, and we would get the letters by that time. By then, we would have forgotten all about the letter. When we received the letters in the mail, this is what I wrote to God:

Dear God

I've been through some challenging times in the past as well as the present. I've left You many times and knowing now in my heart You've never left me, but my question is, where do I go from here? I've learned so much these past few months that have spiritually awakened me. I can no longer live in the past. I have to let go and give it to You and continue to want to live my life bright and happy through You here and now.

I realized I can't do this alone. Jesus, I need You always and forever to guide my steps, correct me where I'm wrong, and make the incorrect choices. Help me in making them correct. Father God, only You are perfect and I'm not. I'm taking each day one day at a time. It is still challenging, but it's a learning process to know I have You by my side, knowing You are in every breath I take, in every walk I make. I'm not alone, and You will put the right people in my life to help me, guide me, love me, and pray for me.

My faith is growing every day, mentally and spiritually. I'm writing this letter to You, God. I'm ready to move forward towards the gift You have given to me, the success that now awaits me. Amen!

We all were given backpacks with gift cards, a diary, etc. I didn't want to leave. I felt free. The feeling was good, something I had never experienced. Before departing the retreat house, we hugged and took pictures. Everyone started to separate, getting in cars, and on the way back to the halfway house. I knew I was heading back to confusion and chaos, and that's what it was at the halfway house.

I stayed in touch with Ann. Whenever I was going through something, I would call her, and we would talk, pray, and also do A.A. over the phone. The ladies from the retreat came to the halfway house, teaching us yoga. When they came, they brought delicious food. This world that I was living in was way different than what I was used to! Even though when chaos was going on within the house, a humbleness came over me. Every time I got upset about something that was going on in the house, I clung to this letter.

This letter made me feel that I had hope, looking toward the gift that God has given me. Everyone gets a gift from God. You have to seek your gift, your success. It's something you see that no one else sees. Open your heart and your mind, set yourself free.

Months have passed. The holiday has come and gone. Rose and I became close. She was the house person of the halfway house. She made sure we did our chores that were assigned to us.

We cooked together on Thanksgiving and Christmas. We would often talk about opening a restaurant together. I never knew that I could go to a party and not drink alcohol. I thought that this party was going to be so boring. I didn't want to go, but anything was better than being in the house, so I went to the Halloween & New Year's Eve party. For New Year's, we were only to stay for 2 hours, but we were having so much fun. One of the staff members from the house came. She called the counselor and asked if we could stay with her till the end.

We went to an N.A. New Year's Eve meeting/party. They had a separate room where you could go to meetings all night. On the other side was the party. They had food, music, and coffee. People were sober and dancing. I had a good time dancing and bringing in the New Year sober, with the other girls that came. I thought to myself, I can party and have fun sober. After the party, we were still roused up. No one wanted to go to bed. We drank sparkling apple cider, played cards, and then went to bed.

One day, Tina, Carla, and I went to the store. On the way back, we were talking. Tina said she wanted to get high. I said, "Do you want to lose everything you worked so hard for to get to this point?" I said, "Tina, you can go back to prison." She said, "Marlene, I don't care. I want to get high." I said to Tina, "Do you think coping with your mother's death is going to make it better? No! It'll make you feel worse. Believe me, I know! You're already beating yourself up because you weren't there when she passed. You were too busy getting high. So now, you want to beat yourself up even more, and making excuses won't help."

I knew she wasn't listening. She had her mind made up. A few weeks later, the house went up in an uproar. It started getting crazy. Tina started sneaking drugs into the house— smoking crack and shooting heroin. One of the girls in her room found two bundles of heroin and flushed them. Everyone was angry. We were all addicts, and to see her and watch her get high was a slap in the face because no one was doing anything. The staff had certain procedures and protocols they had to follow while she was still getting high in the house, nodding and scratching. It made people want to leave that house. It didn't bother me, though, because I wasn't in the room with her any longer, and I didn't deal with her much after she left the room.

I was thinking back when we were in the same room. She was depressed about being in the halfway house and about her mom passing. I would give her scriptures from the Bible for comfort, but she never read them, so I never mentioned anything else about it. This was her battle; she had to fight it. All I could do in morning meditation was to give her words of encouragement, pray for her, and tell her she could get better. I couldn't talk bad about her or degrade her. It could've been me or anyone for that matter. I've seen people come and go and never return because their families are calling to say their daughter died of an overdose. So to talk someone down just wasn't an option. You can't for one moment or one second think you're better than anyone—no, you're not. You're not invisible. You can fall back down. Help reach out your hand. Help pull someone up. Help talk to them. Help reach out. HELP THEM!! If they don't want to be helped, at least you know you did your part, and now it's up to them to ask for help and want the help.

One day I came home from school and Tina was gone. Her officer came and locked her up. I said, "Thank you, Jesus!" She has a chance to try to get sober. Another chance to live. My 4th month was coming up, and I asked if I could leave. I kept hearing excuses why I should stay another month, so I did. I knew it was all about the money. I went for a job interview.

Then my daughter got pulled over in Wayne, NJ. We were all asked for our IDs. My daughter asked, "Why am I being stopped?" The officer said, "I will tell you when I come back." I had nothing to worry about. The officer came back to the car and told me I had a body warrant on me. I said, "WHAT! WHY! WHAT FOR?" I tried to explain to them that I was in a halfway house. I said, "Call them," but they wouldn't because I had a warrant from Freehold, NJ.

Here come two more police cars. The officer claimed we made a wrong turn and the car smelled like marijuana. So, I get arrested. One of the male officers tried to search me. I smacked his hands and said, "Don't fucking touch me!" Boy, was he mad! He turned red, started slobbering from his mouth. I said, "Get a female officer."

The female officer arrived. They searched my daughter's car and found nothing. My daughters, Tiarrah and Ashley, were let go. I told them to call the halfway house to let them know what happened. When you go to rehab and the halfway house, they're supposed to call the courts and let them know where you are so the courts don't put a warrant out for you. Being in the halfway house, I called Freehold Superior Court numerous times to inform them about my whereabouts, and so did the counselor.

After 3-4 hours of sitting, waiting for Freehold to come get me, when I get to Freehold, the correction officer wanted to take my hair loose. I told her, "Hell no! I scraped up change to get my hair done, and you want me to take my hair loose?" I said to the female officer, "the officer just went through my hair in Wayne, NJ. I have nothing in my damn hair. Put me in lockup. I'm not taking my hair down!" After going through the processing, I went upstairs. I was in jail for 2 days. I was let out the day before Thanksgiving. I called the halfway house to inform them I was out. I went to see my family. They had a Thanksgiving party.

I didn't stay long. I got to the halfway house, and they had all my clothes packed, like I did something wrong. The staff tested me by swabbing and taking my urine. They claimed I never called them. I was able to show them what time I called and who I spoke with. One of the other staff members tried to make it seem that she didn't talk to me. I'm thinking to myself, Is this bitch on drugs? Staff needed to swab her ass. My daughter did call and explain what happened.

One of the staff members, Mella, we were getting close. She never doubted me for one second. What I liked about her was that she never showed favoritism, not even with me. We would talk, and all she would do is encourage me. She would always tell me to keep my nose clean. The housing counselor would always shut the house down and take our weekend passes because someone didn't do their chores or didn't wash their dish out, so everyone was being held accountable.

I finally found a job, but it was at night. I didn't think anything of it until I got close to home and called the house counselor to tell her I found a job and would start the next day. When she told me I couldn't take the job, I was so upset. After being in the halfway house all these months without a job, and now you tell me I can't take the job because I have to be in by 10 p.m.? It was so unfair. Another client was able to work late nights. I would hear her coming in the house at 1-1:30 a.m. because she worked with a staff member that was showing favoritism.

I even called the director who owned the halfway house, cursing, crying, angry. I was so upset. Now everyone thought I was going crazy. Then my roommate told me, Maybe this job isn't for you. I had no understanding. All I knew was that I was almost ready to leave this place, broke, no money. After calming down, I wanted to leave, but now they had me by the balls. After going to court, the judge told me I had to complete the program or I was going to jail for some years.

So now I'm no longer a walk-in; I'm mandated until my term is over, which was two months. I have a court date after I leave here. I have to bring my completion certificate. So, sucking up what I had going on, I had to deal with it.

At what point in your life do you say to yourself… I'm DONE. I'm TIRED. Of being told what to do, live life accordingly. Do what you have to do so you don't have to be told what to do. So before you do something wrong, think about the consequences. Just because you didn't get caught the first or second time doesn't mean you won't.

But still, I was determined to have a drink eventually. At some point, I didn't know when. I was still sick mentally. We watched the Whitney Houston movie, and when it was over, we were asked what we would've said to Whitney to make her stop using drugs. I said, "Nothing," because you can't say or do anything to make a person stop. They have to want it. Realizing that her life would've ended because of using, most people won't stop. Who would ever believe that they will die? It's like playing Russian roulette. We all play this game with our lives. It came to my mind a few times while getting high, but I kept doing it.

Most of us say, "Well, at least I'm going out high," but that's not the way to go. I felt like I was cutting myself out of an opportunity to live a real life, the life I deserve to live.

Two months have passed. Rose left the halfway house before she returns home to live with her mother. She felt good to be going home because now she can be the daughter that her mom has been longing for quite some time. Rose felt really good about going home. After Rose left the halfway house, she continued to come to meetings. She even got her brother to come to meetings after he had been struggling with drug addiction. She was really happy that he was finally turning his life around.

My time has come. I called my daughter to come get my belongings. The night before I'm leaving, anticipating the days ahead, and now it's time. Not knowing where I was going, I just wanted to get out of the halfway house. I called my cousin Ju and asked if I could come stay with her until I got things situated. Ju told me to come.

She's my cousin through marriage, Ju is such a sweetheart. She gave up her bedroom for me, gave me money without me even asking. Now it's time for me to go to court and face these charges. I didn't want to go; I'm sober, but thoughts are running through my mind, remembering the last time I went to jail. But I had to go!

I go to court. Before I go in front of the judge, I meet with my lawyer. I handed him my completion papers from the halfway house. We talk, I sign the papers. He says to me, "Marlene, you know you have to do jail time." I said, "Yeah, I know." My heart was beating rapidly! I said to myself, It's only 10 days. I thought about it being 10 slow days, which would feel like forever.

As my lawyer and I approached the courtroom, I was called and sworn in. The judge read off my charges. He asked if I had something to say to the court. I said, "Yes, your honor," then I addressed the court saying how I was very apologetic for my actions. I had never been to rehab or a halfway house before. I also explained my career goals and how I learned so much in both these programs. The judge looked at me and said how he commended me on my completion of both programs. He said, "Marlene, I wish I didn't have to give you 10 days, but I have to."

The officer came over to me, put the handcuffs on, and as I was walking out of the courtroom, he wished me well along my journey of success. The officer put me down in the holding cell. It was so cold, but the wait wasn't long, like before. Before I was in the holding cell, I had on short sleeves. I was so cold, I started crying. Even the tears were cold as they came down my face. The next words that came to me were, God, get me out of this situation.

This time, the process wasn't long. I went upstairs, and my time started. I was out in 3 days. As I look back at that day going to court, there are all types of miracles. We have to ask ourselves all the trials and tribulations we put ourselves through, the grace and mercy that God had set upon us. We shouldn't be here, but we are!

I was angry, mad, and didn't have any understanding. I didn't want to go to meetings or outpatient programs. I said, How can these people tell me what to do? Then I learned about this process in my life. I still think about that cold day in that cold cell, and that was part of my turning point. That's part of my reflection, when I want to look back on things, that will come to mind. I never want to go back to that dark place in my life. There's nothing there: death, institutions, confusion, pain, and agony.

I got out of jail. At first, I was scared to leave the house, scared of the unknown, scared of myself. I fought with myself every day in my mind. I even said to myself, Girl, you're out of the halfway house. LIVE! I found the courage to get out of the house. That job I couldn't get while in the halfway house, I went back there. I got hired on the spot. I even went back to culinary school and graduated in August 2018. My life started to feel good.

All my feelings that were good just went to my gut. I went to an eye doctor to try to learn how to put contacts in my eyes. The optometrist wouldn't allow me to leave unless I was able to put the contacts in. My phone rang, and I answered. It was Mella. She said,

"Marlene, are you sitting down?" I replied, "I'm at the eye doctor's office trying to learn how to put contacts in my eyes." Her reply was, "Are you sitting down?" I replied, "Yes, I'm sitting. What's going on?" She said, "Rose died." My world was gone. I sat in the chair trying to register this in my brain. The question was, What happened? She was so full of life! Nooooo!

I walked out of the eye doctor's office. The receptionist asked if I was okay, but I just kept walking. First, a tear dropped down my face. Mella asked, "Marlene, are you okay?" I replied, "Yeah," in a low voice. She couldn't tell me what happened. The family wouldn't talk about what happened. As I was walking out the door of the doctor's office, which is in the heart of Newark, NJ, it was a very nice day. People were shopping. Downtown Newark is very busy, with people selling things on the sidewalks, hotdog stands were out.

I was so lost at that point, tears were really flowing. People walked past me like it was a normal thing to do. I'm thinking maybe it's better I was having a moment to cry. All the memories came flooding back—how we first met in rehab, how we couldn't get along, until we became best friends once we both ended up in the halfway house.

Weekly visits with my therapist, at the end of my session, she says, "Marlene, write about what life was like in your home as a child." I looked at her and said, "So many bad memories, memories that I would never want to dig up from the grave." She said, "Marlene, something happened to make you use drugs. What happened to you has to be dug up from the grave." She continued to say, "People are most likely to use drugs because of the trauma of their childhood." She said, "Marlene, you have to face those things. Sometimes we choose bad relationships, we make bad decisions, and bad choices. If we're not able to face those issues, we can never recover."

Memories that you try to forget and think that they were forgotten. She said, "For you to completely live free and content with yourself, you have to face those memories so you can heal." I walked outside to light a cigarette, walking to the bus stop, and it started coming to me. Thinking back as far as I can remember, there wasn't any hugging or kissing. If it was, I didn't see much of it at all. I remember it was dysfunctional—anger and abuse. I saw them have good times, like parties... kids were seen but weren't heard.

The description of dysfunctional was seeing a lot of my father cheating on my mom. He used to take me to other women's houses. The fun I had with my father was when he did drive, he would sit me on his lap while driving. I would steer with his help, of course. He was my hero growing up. I felt safe with him, and I was full of life. I was a tomboyish type of girl. When he was home, he would put me to bed, tuck me in, and give me a hug and a kiss goodnight.

My father never hit or beat me, and if he did hit me, then he would take me out for ice cream and apologize. Being 5 years old, innocent and full of life, I played with boys, got dirty, and played with garden snakes. My mom had two miscarriages. One of them, we were in the house. She told me to go get my aunt, my father's youngest sister, who lived behind us. My aunt called the ambulance. The street we lived on was quiet with good neighbors. We could leave our doors and windows open, when we moved.

We lived in the apartment building my aunt and her husband owned. My aunt was my father's other sister. She was the second to the oldest. When we moved in, it wasn't too far from our grandparents; it was either down the street or around the corner. Growing up, I was always in the hospital getting stitches. I had stitches in my head, my tongue, above the left eyebrow. I got burnt on my stomach bad on the old-fashioned floor radiator that I don't remember. I still have the scars today.

We lived across the street from the beach in Long Branch, NJ— that's where I grew up. In the summertime, you could always hear the kids outside playing, the music from the boardwalk. Some hot summer nights, my parents and I would go to the boardwalk to get ice cream. We were able to leave our doors open. The street we lived on was quiet, and it seemed everyone was nice. It was a good neighborhood. Those were the days I didn't mind remembering.

Winter was really bad when it snowed; no one could get out their doors. In the '70s, you had to shovel your way out the door. I remember a big icicle would hang from the edges of the roof.

I learned early how to steal and lie. My parents would get into fights and put me in the middle, asking me which one of them I wanted to go live with. I used to be scared to say who. My mom would look at me with her big, bubbly eyes, and my father would stare at me like, "You better say you'll come stay with me." Can you imagine being a little kid and having to make a decision between two adults? On the other hand, at any other time, you weren't supposed to be seen or heard. Now, ain't that some shit?

When my father and mother would fight, my mom would call the police, or sometimes my aunt would. My father's middle sister had no children; she had it all—a good husband, nice cars, and always dressed nice. They did nothing. The officers who came did nothing because they went to school with my father. The officers would tell him to take a walk. In those days, nobody did anything; everyone turned their heads.

I remember this family that lived across the street. The mother was 400–500 lbs, and the father was 150 lbs. He would beat her so bad. I also saw it happen in my grandparents' house. It was so scary, but the next day, my grandparents would take it out on me. They wouldn't let me in their house and wouldn't speak to my mom. Then, when I was allowed over there, I would be called fat or told, "You're going to be fat like your mother." They would be mad at my aunt too, but not for too long. But me? I was being tortured.

I told my mother what was going on, and she said nothing. The family was scared of my grandfather. Whatever he said went. Going over my grandparents' house, if my grandfather was asleep, no one could even walk down the hall passing his room. My grandmother was scared of him. And if you got a beating by him, you got beat with this razor strap. It was a leather belt-like strap that he cut into strings, and when he hit you, all the straps were sure to hit you all over. My cousin Danny used to get beat all the time. He was either always getting expelled from school or doing things he had no business doing.

Danny and Sue were my father's sister's children—my father's older sister—and my grandparents took them to raise them both. I remember when my grandfather told me not to ride my big wheel in the road. One day, he came around the corner of the street we resided on and caught me riding my big wheel in the street. He was chasing me with that razor strap. I rode that big wheel so fast, trying to get home. He didn't catch me. I was so scared (it's funny now, but it sure wasn't funny then).

I burnt my parents' bed up. My mother wouldn't let me go outside to play with other kids, so I got bored. I was running back and forth with little glasses of water, trying to put the fire out. Back in the '70s, all we had was outside; there were no video games or cell phones. TV was just TV—there was no internet or cable, not even cartoons. Cartoons were only in the morning, so hearing all the kids playing outside, I wanted to go outside.

I remember her trying to burn my finger on the stove. I fought by kicking and biting her, just the thought of getting burnt and thinking of the pain. She got tired; she was pregnant at the time with my twin brothers. I wasn't being monitored. I was 7 years old—what do you think a bored 7-year-old is going to do? So, of course, I got punished, which I felt was already happening just by being born. I was never allowed to go outside.

My dad was working in the Meadowlands with horses. He was also a barber. He would trim the end of my hair. My mom wasn't allowed to hit or beat me then. I remember him coming home and asking me what happened. As soon as I told him, he would beat her up. I remember him saying, "Don't put your hands on my daughter."

I was Daddy's little girl, and when he was home, he would smoke marijuana and drink alcohol, like Night Train or Thunderbird, with me. This was the first time I was introduced to drugs. My mom wasn't allowed to say anything; it continued until one day I went to school and said something to my teacher. I thought it was cool until my parents were called in for a conference. They clearly said that it wasn't true, and nobody investigated anything. He whooped her when she was 7-8 months pregnant with my brothers, but she was stupid— she stayed.

The reason why I would never know, I witnessed him kicking her and beating her while pregnant. Before she got pregnant with my brothers she was pregnant and had a miscarriage, this is how I grew up in an abusive home year after year! during that time I was also being raped by a family member by my cousin Danny I tried to tell but no one listened, my mom was asleep, sleep to everything that was going on, I started acting out, getting in trouble in school, fighting I was the only child for 8 years before my twin brothers were born in 1977.

All I had to play with was my cousin. She was one year younger than I was, my father's younger sister's daughter. Most of the time, we played together, but we would fight—I'm mean, scratch each other in the face. Sometimes she'd win, sometimes I would. I guess that's why she would never let me outside to play, but that is what kids do. She had no siblings; it was just us two that kept each other company. Her sister was born after my brothers.

I was in second grade, fighting the sixth-grader. I was so angry! I didn't know God; I was too young to understand who He was. Yes, I went to church, and every Sunday my mom and grandmother would cook big Sunday dinners. They would start cooking Sunday dinner on Saturday, and you couldn't clean or wash clothes on Sundays. We had family outings; we had good times as well. But if I had to weigh out the good from the bad, it was bad. The good was when my mom would leave my father. We'd go to my grandmother's house in Red Bank, N.J. It gave me a chance to see her. The bad was when she went back to him.

My grandmother wanted to raise me. All she kept saying was that my mother wouldn't let her. When my grandmother would come to Long Branch, my mother wouldn't allow her to see me. How I learned to lie was because whenever my mother's siblings would come over, she would tell me to tell them she wasn't home. I wasn't allowed to open the door. Sometimes I was allowed to hang out with my cousins from Red Bank, but not often. I never wanted to go back home.

My grandmother would take me out shopping when I could go with her, when i got home my mother would take my clothes and wear them, me and my mother was almost the same size I had tities and ass and back in the day sears was the store or my aunt would come get me and take me to Macy's she had no children, she was my mother sister.

Whoever is reading this book, I'd like for you to take a moment to reflect on your life and never take it for granted. I have seen many pass away through this disease of alcoholism and addiction. I'm one of many that made it through God's grace and mercy. I truly believe He has a plan for me to carry out, and you will too, once you overcome your fears and regrets. We can no longer go back and fix the mess we made of ourselves, so please get help before it's too late. Once it's too late, you can't come back from the dead and ask for another chance. See a therapist, talk to someone, break the chains, and stop holding your family hostage.

I held my family hostage—my children—because I didn't know how to be a parent. I used drugs, couldn't pay rent, so we were mostly evicted. I had to send my kids to live elsewhere. It wasn't fair to them. The chains of my captivity had me so blind, and I continue to ask how to better myself so I can be a better person, inside and out. They hurt too, especially when they have to bury you.

I don't want it to be me. I don't want anything else to ever haunt me or keep me hostage. I hurt my kids. I was 16 when I had my first daughter. When the nurse brought her to me, she was so tiny, all wrapped up in the blanket. I unwrapped her, counting her little fingers and toes, promising her I would never let anyone harm her.

Did I keep that promise? Sure, I did. But I didn't keep myself from harming her or my second child. I wasn't realizing that hurting people was a problem. But it is—and it was for me. I was letting others, as well as myself, hold me back from a great life I know I can have, the life I deserve—and you can have it too.

Serenity is to surrender. Surrender to your higher power, to whomever you see as your God. We all need somebody greater than ourselves. This is why I'm writing. I no longer want to blame anyone else for my falling grace. I've started a new life. No more will I keep holding myself hostage. I'm able to breathe and think now. It's time for me to let it all go. I want to tell you what happened in my life. Coming Out of the Woods gives me a clearer path to victory!

On how I became who I was and who I am today! The question is am I different from others that have been abused or raped and molested? People have told their stories and wrote books.

As I continue to write I feel that mine is not much of a difference. We all share the same abuse, some of us recover, some have died and just couldn't handle what has happened to them as a child. It has also driven us to a mental breakdown, some of us had no way out and yes I can agree and relate to the pain and hurt, we are left abandoned, the guilt. This is my story, I began to think it was ok and it was a natural thing to do. So I started acting out with other kids.

When my parents would take me to their friends house while they partied, I would be in the room with their kids trying to have sex with their son, they had a son and 2 daughters, they told on me, nothing was done about it, I'm thinking that i was in trouble, no it was just swept under the rug, like everything else, this was one of those night that my father tucked me in and kissed me good night.

2 years passed. Christmas Eve, my parents went to the store and left me and my brothers with a family friend. I was 10 years old, and my brothers were 2 years old. He sexually approached me, asking me to come sit on his lap. I told him I was telling my parents when they returned home. My mom was the first one in the house when I told her. She replied by saying I deserved it and that I was fresh. It felt like someone stabbed me in the heart. My own mother said this to me.

My cousin came to stay with us for a short time, and then she was gone. She never looked back. I missed her when she left. I guess it was too much chaos going on. I often wonder if she would have called just to say, "Marlene, hold your head up, keep moving forward." I never had anyone who really believed in me or encouraged me to look beyond my dreams and goals. I don't even remember having dreams or goals.

Something started to change in me. During these years, I was hearing how mothers were killing their children and putting them in ovens. I even remember being 13 years old, standing at my parents' door with a knife. I opened the door quietly and saw them both asleep. I said, "This is my chance." I've always wished them to die, but they still manage to wake up every fucking day! As I was standing at the door, a thought came over me: where will I go? Who would take me? I thought about running away many times. The question is, where will I go? I closed the door. A thought never crossed my mind about jail. I just wanted them gone, but I couldn't do it! The anger and the pain!

My father used to come in the house at 3 or maybe 4 AM in the morning, ordering me to get out of bed to fix him something to eat. He would always say to me that he wasn't my father. Some of those mornings, my mother would get out of bed, and she would say, "Marlene, go back to bed." When she got out of bed, I could hear them fighting and arguing. I just couldn't go back to sleep; I had to be up by 6 AM. Some days, I would fall asleep in school. Some mornings, she didn't get out of bed; I guess she didn't feel like fighting. That stuck in my mind. Then, if he's not my father, then who is my father? My mother would always say, "Ignore him; he is your father."

One summer night, my parents went out. I had just put my brothers to sleep when I heard a knock on the door. The girl from across the street, who was a little older than me, told me to come take a look at her clubhouse. I said okay; it was just across the street. I got to the basement, and I was attacked by three guys. One held my legs, the other one held an ax to my throat, while the other one got on top of me and raped me. I don't know if it was rape; he couldn't get his penis inside because I held my legs really tight. He ejaculated between my thighs. When they let me go, I ran home. My parents were home, and my heart was pounding. As I walked up the stairs, I could hear that my parents were home. I was like, "SHIT! FUCK!" I just sat on the stairs when they opened the door. I tried explaining what happened, but they didn't want to hear anything. I got beat so badly with an extension cord.

The following month, I was pregnant. My mother took me to get an abortion. After two weeks, my mother and her friend Ann—my mother and her family all grew up together— took me to the doctor. While at the doctor's office, I told the doctor what happened. I told anyone who would listen, and all they did was listen. I even called DYFS because I got beat with an extension cord, but they did nothing.

I was doing so horribly in school; I never brought home good grades. So then I knew I wasn't going to be let outside for the whole summer. If she did let me outside, I wouldn't be allowed anywhere off the porch. I could just watch the kids play. If my brothers got to my homework and ripped it up, her words were, "Stop leaving your homework around." Even if my brothers would run around and mess up the house after I cleaned it, the house was never clean to her satisfaction because they tore it the fuck up. I couldn't hit them; I had no control. Taking up sports or going on field trips was not an option!

So, at 14 or 15 years of age in middle school, I found friends. We all became really close. My cousin, my father's oldest sister's younger daughter, and I would skip school, go to stores, and steal. We would go hook up with guys from out of town.

Their house became our hideout until it was time to go home in the 80s. We didn't have the internet to meet guys; it was all by word of mouth. If you knew guys, they would bring their friends. All we had was a landline phone. I went and stole a phone so I could talk to people once my mother went to sleep. I was hiding it in my closet. I had to be in bed by 6 PM, so I would wait until 8 PM to make sure she was asleep. Sometimes I would fall asleep on the phone talking until I heard that noise that came over the phone; it woke me up. I'd get up and put it back in my closet.

I got caught one day by my father. We pretended to have been in school. One day when I got home, he said, "How was school today?" I replied it was fine. He said, "I know you didn't go to school today." He said, "I'm not going to tell your mother." I side-eyed him. My cousin YoYo looked at me, and I looked back at her. She was now living downstairs from me. My father's middle sister and her husband moved out; they still owned the building we lived in, but I knew one day he was going to get mad at me and then bring it up so she could whoop my ass. Sometimes he would instigate things just so she would beat my ass.

One evening, while we were sitting at the dinner table, he told me to get up and get him butter out of the refrigerator. I replied, "You're sitting next to the refrigerator." The way my mother looked at me, I knew I better get up. I cut my eyes at him, and all I knew was that I was getting slapped by my mother. All that thinking that I was Dad's little girl definitely went out the window once my brothers were born. Times like this were when I wished them DEAD!

One day, I went to the mall with my friends. We were all going to steal. It was a Sunday afternoon. I lied and said, "Can I go to the mall with my friend's mom?" At first, my mother said no, but I convinced her that my friend's mother was going to drop me off. I just had to meet them at the mall, and Yo-Yo took the bus.

The first time I was allowed to go out, I was never allowed outside, especially on a Sunday. I got caught stealing. My mother and my aunt, his middle sister, came to pick me up from the county jail where the police were holding me. I thought I was in trouble. I told the officer they could keep me; I didn't want to go home. The officer tried to give me a lecture, and in my mind, I said, "Fuck the lecture, keep me here."

When I got home, she just took the clothes that I stole. I went stealing because I got tired of going to school with bell-bottom pants on. I would wear leg warmers to hide the bottom of my pants. I never remembered my mother buying me anything from the mall; she would go to a cheap store or J.J. Newberry's. I used to get teased. We stole clothes, Polaroid cameras, and film. My friend Tanisha's mother didn't dress her well either. She took me to a drug-infected area to let my father know that I was out—an area we were taught we could never cross any blocks or go anywhere near. We better not have asked why; "why" wasn't a question!

He said to my mother, "That's your daughter." The next day in school, they asked what I stole. I said, "Baby socks." They laughed at me. "Baby socks?!" They were cracking up. They asked, "Why would you steal baby socks?" I said, "Shit, I don't know; I thought I could fit them."

One afternoon, the phone rang. I answered the phone, and the person asked for my father, so I went to go get him. When I pushed the door, it was locked. When I went to push the door, it opened just enough for me to see that he was in the room with his friend, shooting up drugs. It was the first time in my life seeing such a thing. I ran to tell my mother, but she said, "Sit your ass down."

Life for me started to spiral out of control. My cousin, whom I grew up with, had moved fifteen to twenty minutes away. She stayed in school; she never was a problem, not like me, but she never got treated the way I was treated. My grandfather passed away. I guess my grandfather was the rock of the family. He was a very mean man.

One evening, my grandfather came home and didn't see my cousins—the ones he was raising—were in the house. I saw him chase my grandmother up the steps with a gun because they weren't home. When he came home, everyone had to be in the house. My grandmother was screaming; I really thought he was going to shoot her. Whoever was in the house, we all were screaming and crying. Then

I remember them walking in the house, remembering that razor strap; he tore their asses up. If my grandfather was coming around the corner and you saw him, you had to run in the house. You had to beat him in the house; you never knew when he was coming home.

After he passed away, at the funeral, my mother tried to take him out of the casket. Everyone started yelling, "JEAN, STOP!" Some people started to walk out of the church. It wasn't long after my grandfather passed away that the whole family started to separate. It was like a bad plague that entered that family. My cousin Sue went to jail.

When she came home from prison, she got pregnant with her first child. She was in her 30s, and everyone was so happy. After she gave birth, the baby died a month after he was born. I learned she had AIDS. I went to see her in the hospital. She had always been thin; she was now like a skeleton with skin. She died a year later after her baby passed away. I got pregnant at 16 years old. When my mother found out, she started kicking and stomping me. My father eventually left us all and married someone else. When he left my mother, she said it was all my fault because I got pregnant.

My mother started drinking more than usual; she would drink only on the weekends. She and her co-worker would get off work, play music, and fry fish on Fridays—lots of it too. It was 1985 when he got married; he married his wife right next door at his mother's (my grandmother's) house on the front patio for everyone to see! When we walked out the door that day, it was heart-wrenching to see the man she'd been with all these years—the man that beat her, cheated on her, degraded her and us—and now he was marrying someone else. Was that the will of God? Removing him out of our lives.

My mother then met a guy who treated us like his kids. Things were a little different in the home. I was three months pregnant when I met Samuel's brother, Marcus, from Asbury Park, NJ. He was in a gang called the O.P.G. I went to school for pregnant teenagers. One day, my mother and my aunt asked me who I was pregnant by. She never asked me before; I was five to six months along. I made up some random guy because when I was asked, I was shocked that she wanted to know. My aunt, my father's middle sister, said Daren called me and said he was the baby's father. I had my back turned, my eyes got so big, and I held my breath, then exhaled softly. My aunt asked, "IS HE THE FATHER?!" I said yes softly. Daren was my aunt's husband's brother. He would always come up on holidays or during the summer. He was much older than I was, and from being a young girl, I'd always had a crush on him.

He came to live with us; he had a job. My parents were always taking in boarders, especially in the summer when the racetrack came; that's how they made extra money. My father worked with horses. I remember getting up at 3 AM on the weekends with my father and hanging out with him at the stables in Colts Neck, NJ, or the Meadowlands when I was 8 or 9 years old. Daren had thick curly hair and a bronze complexion; he was a handsome guy, but he was always getting into trouble with the law. I remember one day he was supposed to have gone to the store. He came running around the corner with ten Puerto Ricans chasing him and his cousin; they were fighting with sticks. After that day, I never saw him again. My aunt's husband sent him back to Atlantic City.

After I had given birth to my first daughter, Lateria, in 1986, when the nurse brought her to me, I unwrapped her and counted her fingers and toes. As I looked down at her, she had straight black hair; she looked just like an Indian doll. I said that I would always protect her. My aunt, my father's older sister, named her and became her godmother. After two months, I went back to public school, stayed in school, and got a job. My first job was at Roy Rogers. I was really determined to graduate high school and be a good mother. Then I found a better job where I was putting components in boards for radios and refrigerators.

I would leave school at 2:38 PM, run to the bus stop, and had to be at work by 3:30 PM; the bus came at 3 PM. I got off work at 11:30 PM. I would have to go home, make bottles, and pack my daughter's bag at night, getting her ready to go to the babysitter, which was my grandmother—my father's mother. When my mother would get off work, she would pick her up. When my father left, my mother started to drink very heavily. The guy she was dating treated my brothers and me like his own, and he was happy to be a grandfather to my daughter. Even though he couldn't replace my father, he was there.

Coming home from work, I hated it. I would stand in the hallway before entering the house, putting my ear to the door because I knew if she was drinking, there would be music playing. That meant that she was up. I opened the door to the house and walked in. Everything was quiet for a moment. The more she drank, I knew it was going to be problems. She started to accuse me of wanting her boyfriend. She would kick me out sometimes and throw my clothes down the steps. I would go to my grandmother's house late at night with my daughter. I would go to school and fall asleep. My mother would get phone calls from my teachers; they were wondering why I was falling asleep in school. My mother told me I had to stop working because I wasn't focused in school.

I said to myself, "If you let me go to bed at night and stop kicking me out all times of the night, I can get sleep." I didn't stay in school. Three of my friends and I dropped out of school and started Brookdale College the following year to get our G.E.D. One day, we were going to hang out in Asbury Park. The wheel on the stroller broke. I asked my friends Vee, Tanisha, and Yo-Yo to help me carry it. They were saying no; it was heavy. Then I knew I couldn't hang out with them much; I had a baby, and they didn't. Eventually, we all dropped out of school. All my friends started having babies, and I would always have my daughter with me.

My mother's boyfriend broke up with her, and she kept accusing me of wanting to sleep with him. Sometimes I would go stay at my friend Vee's house; her parents were always nice to me. I continued to see Marcus, and my friend Vee started dating his friend. We became the O.P.G.s (Original Play Girls), and they were the Original Play Boys. Of course, I was 16. My neighbor across the street, Maree, and then I met Mary through Maree. They had no kids and would try to get me into bars, putting makeup on my face; I looked like a clown.

We would go to a bar in Red Bank, where most of my mother's family were from. Trying to get into the bar, they knew who I was. They would ask me, "Are you Jean's daughter?" I'd say, "Yeah." They would tell me they knew I wasn't old enough to be in there. I had to sit in the car until the bar was over. After that, I never went back. I wasn't drinking.

One evening, I went to hang out with Maree and Mary. We were sitting at Maree's house, drinking Bacardi and Coke. I got so wasted. I had my daughter with me, and they helped me walk across the street. They helped me up the stairs, knocked on the door, and heard my mother coming. They sat Lateria on my lap and ran. My mother opened the door, took Lateria from me, and told me to go to bed. When I woke up, I banged my eye on a floor model old TV.

The next morning, my eye was black and blue. I put steak on my eye and had a hangover. When I finally got up, Lateria was dressed, and my room was cleaned. All my mother said was, "You came in here stumbling; don't take the baby out with you like that." After that, every weekend, my house became the party house. It turned into a slumber party because my mother wouldn't let anyone leave. I never thought my life had intoxicated males or females; if you had keys, you weren't leaving. The next day, my mother would go outside, and there would be liquor bottles on the porch. I never thought that my life was becoming unmanageable.

Me and Marcus broke up. He was living with me, got a job working construction, and brought a car, leaving it at my house while he went to work. I didn't know how to drive, but I drove it. I ran over the sidewalk and kept driving it until I learned how to drive. We got into a huge argument and decided to go our separate ways. For me, life went on, but we both remained friends.

My mother started dating another guy who was a little younger than her. He seemed to be cool too, but she started accusing me of wanting him. That relationship didn't last too long; he moved out because he couldn't take her accusations. When he moved, he said, "Whenever your mother kicks you out, you can come to my apartment."

One evening, I was getting off work when she started arguing with me. She began throwing my clothes down the stairs. I packed up my daughter, put her in her stroller, and walked over to his house. It was late, around 12 AM. I thought about going over to my grandmother's house; she lived next door, but her house was crowded. So, I went over to his house. He gave his bed to me and Lateria to sleep in. He left, and when he came back, the birds were chirping.

He and his friends came with drugs. He had cocaine, crack, and heroin. I asked if I could try it. At first, he said no, but then he did allow me to try it. I sniffed cocaine and smoked crack. At first, I didn't like it. I was 17 years old now. I didn't do heroin; I was scared of that. I had seen what it did to people—nodding and scratching. I'd seen people shooting it. One thing he said to me was, "If you keep doing it, you will get addicted." I said, "No, not me!"

The next thing you know, I was going to Asbury Park with Mary and Maree every weekend, buying cocaine. Then we started lacing the cigarettes with cocaine. At that time, I thought it was fun and cool. The guys we were getting our drugs from started hanging out with us. The friends I went to school with didn't hang out much anymore; they were in love or had their own things going on. Maree lived across the street from where I stayed, and her family moved onto my street. When she was 10 years old, when I was allowed outside, we jumped double Dutch, played softball, and kickball. We had a big field in the middle of our block. I would ask to go to her house because I needed help with homework, just to get out of the house.

My daughter Lateria was about to turn a year old. I called her father to see if he was coming to her birthday party. He said he was coming and that he wouldn't miss her party. The day before, he claimed he couldn't make it. I was so upset.

Weeks later, Vee and I decided to go to Atlantic City to pay my daughter's father a visit. The reunion was nice; it was also nice to see him after spending a few hours together. Vee and I missed the last bus and found ourselves stranded in Atlantic City. I called Darren to inform him we missed the last bus. He and his cousin came to get us. Darren snuck us into his basement. His mother knew we were down there; she said, "I know you got them girls down there." He was like, "Shhhhh." We slept down there until the next day. The next day, she went to work. As Darren and I started talking, he wanted me to come live in the same house with his mother. After talking, we had sex.

A month later, I realized that I missed my menstruation. I told Vee I wanted to keep my baby. As I thought long and hard, living with my mother was already a nightmare. It was so bad that when I brought foods that I liked, my brothers would eat them. As soon as I would say something, there would go an argument. I was working and getting assistance, but she wanted half of everything. I couldn't buy what I liked or have what I wanted to eat.

After I told Darren I was pregnant, he offered for me and my daughter to move to Atlantic City. I couldn't see how that would work; he didn't have a job and had no goals. I figured I was already raising Lateria by myself, and I couldn't afford another child, so I made an appointment to get an abortion.

Two months later, Lloyd just started stopping by, hanging out with me and picking me up from work. I thought it was just him being nice. He'd been my neighbor since him and his family moved across the street. We went to school together, and we even worked at Roy Rogers together. Months later, we were dating, and I got pregnant with my other daughter. Of course, I stopped partying. Things got really bad at home; my mother would try to fight me.

She would say, "Your baby is going to be ugly." When she would throw me out, I would either go to his house or a family member's house. I really didn't want to keep her because I was already a single mother. When I discussed my options, he begged me to keep her, and we decided to raise her together.

After three months of being pregnant, he now wanted to cheat on me. I told him, "Shit, I want to have sex with other people too." I told him I was going to get rid of the baby so we could go our separate ways. I took all the clothes he had at my house and burned them right in front of my house so he could see. I made the appointment, and he found out. The day before, he came to me and begged me to keep his first child, so I did. Things got better.

I had to quit my job; I was always sick from the pregnancy. This was a difficult pregnancy for me; I had to keep running to the hospital. My baby barely ever moved, but she was fine. After I had my second daughter in February of 1989, she was born a day before her father's birthday. She was so adorable, with little lips and long fingers. She had feet like her father. My oldest daughter was a happy baby; she hardly ever cried and was potty trained at one and a half years old. My second daughter was a hip baby; I could never put her down. When I thought she was asleep, when I went to lay her down, she would wake up. I knew then I didn't want any more kids.

When I did leave her in the house, my mother would say, "Oh no, take that hollering ugly baby with you." She would always say, "Lateria don't have a father." She thought my second daughter's father was going to mistreat her. I guess it was guilt on her part. I thought about the way I was mistreated by my father, who said I wasn't his child.

A year later, I couldn't take my mother's abuse anymore. My cousin Tammy said I could move in with her; she already had three kids of her own. Lloyd and I started making plans for our future. I told him I was moving in with my cousin to save money so we could get our own apartment. But it didn't take me long to get back to partying. I was 19 years old now, and I could get into bars.

One evening, Lloyd came to visit. He would never want to stay the night with me; he would come, pop in, then leave. I started cheating. One evening, he came over, and the guy I was seeing was there. He knew about Lloyd. Cam walked up behind me to hug me, and I jumped away from him. Lloyd saw it but said nothing.

So, I went to go see Lloyd and took Essence with me. He left and didn't come back until the morning. Then I knew he had someone else, and he had another baby on the way. I walked away, but I was hurt. The only thing I asked of him was to spend her birthday with her and help me with holidays; he couldn't even do that.

As for me and Cam, we stopped seeing each other. He wanted me to tell Lloyd right then that we were seeing each other. I didn't! I couldn't! Lloyd would see me walking in the snow or rain with my daughter and drive right past us. I was so upset because regardless of whether he was mad at me, he should have put his daughter and Lateria in the car.

After living with my cousin Tammy, I thought she was paying the rent. Maybe a week later, she told me we were about to be homeless. At this time, we were living in Asbury Park. I refused to go back to live with my mother, so I called welfare. They put me and my kids in a hotel.

One day, I went to visit my mother; my father was there. I said, "Y'all back together?" She said no, she just let him stay the night. My mother eventually moved to Red Bank, and I felt I had no choice but to move back in with her. I didn't stay long; I got accepted into Linkage, a program for mothers and children. We had to stay there for nine months to a year before we got our Section 8.

At that time, I was dating my latest husband, Magary. He never knew I was doing drugs. He would always say he wanted to adopt Lateria. After being in Linkage, we had visitation hours, which were only on the weekends. Clarice, Tammy, Precious, and others would sneak out to go to the bars. Sneaking back in wasn't fun. The office sometimes would pull random urine tests.

One evening, I got called to the office. I was asked to give a urine sample, and I knew it was going to be dirty because they saw me hanging out with this lady named Deloris. The office sent me to outpatient treatment. I told them I didn't have a problem; I was in denial. So, I stopped hanging out with Deloris. I couldn't afford to get caught with another dirty urine test. If I did, I was getting kicked out, so I stayed on the straight and narrow.

One day, I went to visit my grandmother, my father's mother. I learned that my father had moved back into my grandmother's house. That's when I would take my daughter to see him. That day, I learned he had AIDS, and the same day my grandmother told me she had cancer. I was so lost for words. I was in my 20s; I couldn't believe what I was hearing. I went to my mother and said, "That day I saw my father in the house—DID YOU SLEEP WITH HIM?" She replied, "NO! He just spent the night." I thought to myself, thank your lucky stars he was trying to give you that shit! I really felt bad for my grandmother. She was a goodhearted person. I had seen people take advantage of her after my grandfather passed away. She finally got her license and kept my grandfather's car until she got it.

She would drive herself to the store. She was feeling good about herself. Somehow, my father ended up in jail. From there, he went to prison. I was still living in Linkage when my aunt, my father's youngest sister, called me. I don't remember how I got there, but I ended up at the prison hospital. My aunt stopped me at the door of the hospital and said, "He doesn't look like he did the last time you saw him." She explained to me that he was on morphine and could hear what I was saying. She said, "DON'T MAKE NO FACIAL EXPRESSION." I replied, "OK."

I had no idea what to expect. As I walked into the hospital room, he had no skin on his face; he looked like something out of a scary movie! I couldn't keep my composure. I screamed and started crying. My aunt had to pull me out of the room. After that, the nightmares started. I just couldn't get it out of my mind.

I finally received my Section 8 voucher, and I was looking forward to moving into my apartment. I had been with Magary off and on. I didn't go to my father's funeral, but my mother did receive his flag from my father's sisters, my aunts. After getting my keys to my apartment, I was never there; I stayed at my mother's house. Magary asked me one evening, "Why are you here? Why are you not home?" I used the excuse that I had no furniture. He said, "Go home; you haven't been there!"

At this time, I was getting high. I was running to New York, picking up packages, and I was getting paid really well in product. It would be gone by the next day. I never wanted to sleep, but nevertheless, he came back to pick me and the kids up. When I walked into my apartment, it was furnished with a white leather sofa. In the kitchen was a square glass table with chairs. I already had beds and dressers. I thought, "There's no excuse now."

After a few months, he started to see people. He began to give me that look—the look when they know but don't know. One day, he asked me if I was using drugs. I lied and said no! He said, "Get in the car." I got in the car, and he was taking me to the doctor's office to get a drug test. Somehow, as an addict, I lied my way out of it. I somewhat felt like this was my life—a life of misery. But I knew what I wanted, and I knew what I had to do. I just wasn't ready to stop.

One day, my cousin Tammy came by with her girlfriend. They would stay with me from time to time, and we would get high at night because I knew that Magary was home asleep. Magary never used drugs or drank.

Now I see them tricking and making money—something I said I'd never do—and I did. At first, they were giving me things, sharing, but then they started to penny pinch. I decided to start going out on my own. The guys I met, I just gave them my phone number. I no longer had to go on the streets, and some guys just didn't want anything but a place to get high and kept sending you out to get it. Of course, I brought them back what they wanted, but I was then pocketing the rest.

Throughout my 20s and into my 30s, getting high cost me nothing: in and out of jail, prisons, fines, and restitution; getting evicted. During the time I had to go back to my mother's house, I just accepted the abuse. Now I'm being called a junkie. I went to prison in 1995 in Clinton, NJ. When you go to prison, they run all types of tests. One thing for sure is that I didn't think about what the outcome of my life would be while out there in those streets, getting high and selling my spirit and my soul.

My test results came back after seeing women in prison with AIDS who didn't have families, and I was afraid. The guard shackled me, put me in a van, and drove me over. They unshackled me and had me waiting in the waiting area. My name was called: "Marlene Dotts." I got up and walked into the office. By this time, my heart was in my stomach. He looked at me and told me to have a seat. Anxiety kicked in. The doctor said, "Your test results came in." He opened my folder, looked at me, then looked back down. He said, "All your test results came back negative." I felt like dancing! A sigh of relief came over me; my heart found its way back in my chest.

That night, that very night, I was in bed praying to God, thanking Him for saving me. I even started to read the Bible. As I closed my eyes,

I said, "Jesus, if you stood in front of me right now, I won't be scared." I opened my eyes after having this conversation, and lo and behold, one of the ladies who was in the same dome as I was standing over me. She was Caucasian, had blonde hair, and wore a long white pajama gown. I trembled and started to shake; I was so startled. I said, "Girl, why the hell are you standing at the foot of my bed, looking like Jesus?" She was cracking up. She said, "I was on my way to the bathroom." I looked up and said to Jesus, "Nope, I ain't ready to meet you."

I still read the Bible; I didn't really know the meaning of it. I guess it was to read to pass the time. During that time, I was writing Magary letters, but he was not responding to my letters.

I got out in 1996. My dearest grandmother, my mother's mother, allowed me to live with her. I was only allowed to visit my kids. I came home on parole, and Magary started to come back around.

He told me he came to check on the kids while I was away. Magary was Haitian, a really nice guy. He asked me to marry him, so I did to get his green card. I said, "What the heck? We've been off and on for the past six years." It didn't take me long to start using again, but this time I wasn't selling my body; I got a job. It was at Boston Market. I started stealing from my job; I knew the whole menu, the costs, and taxes. Chris worked in the back, and as he would bring the food up to the serving line, I would stuff money in his pocket. By the end of the night, I was stealing $300 to $500 a day. That's how I met Chris. He would give me rides home; he became my drug dealer and then my lover.

I was still on parole. Chris and I started living in rooming houses. I would get urine from people and freeze it. When it was time for me to go to parole, I'd let it thaw, warm it, and then I would shove it inside of me to get my body temperature up. Sometimes my parole officer would just pop up. One morning, my parole officer came to get me. I had a bottle on me, but at that time, I just didn't care. She said my urine came back dirty. I didn't have much longer on parole, and she locked me up.

Magary came to see me. He said, "Now I can sleep at night because I know you're here." After that, he died of a brain aneurysm. I was no good; he was my best friend, and now he's gone. What have I done? I couldn't even go to his funeral; I was in jail. He left me money in the bank, but I did no good with it.

When I got back out, Chris and I were selling drugs and using to the point we started living in my mother's basement. It was a nice, finished basement with 3-4 rooms. One day, my grandmother said, "I'm sending you to Florida, you and your kids." She called my cousin, who was selling fish and chips in the mall. I learned that my grandmother was sick; she got diagnosed with cancer and passed away. She was two weeks from being 89 years old. My family sent me tickets for me and my kids to come to the funeral.

After the funeral, I went back to Florida. I got a court notice in the mail to go to court; I was facing eviction. My kids wanted to go back home anyway. We packed up. Chris went to Georgia to visit his children, and we were to meet back up in Jersey. I got high with the money I had, so now I was stuck in Florida. I had family there, but I didn't ask for help. I met up with some people who told me I had to get up early in the morning in order to sign up to work, and at the end of the day, I would get paid.

I found a safe place for us to sleep; it was inside of a truck trailer. I couldn't sleep; I had to keep an eye on my kids while they rested. The next morning, I got up and went to the place. I told my kids, "No matter what, you wait for me here. I'm going to do this job to get money so we can go home."

While I was there, I was talking to this white lady who offered for me and the kids to come to her home. We showered, ate, and then fell asleep. When I woke up, she had the kids, but then I felt like she didn't want me to leave. Eventually, she let me use her phone. At first, she wouldn't let me use it. The guy who gave me a ride when I first came to Florida was named Mike. I called him, and he came. He put me and my kids on the train back to New Jersey. I reached out to this lady and thanked her, but I lost contact. I stayed in contact with Mike.

When I got back to Jersey, it was winter, and I didn't have a coat yet. Both my brothers were in jail, so I borrowed one of their coats. The next day, she came to look for me and snatched it right off me. I looked at her and said with a smile, "You're still the same." I said to her, "Oh, by the way, I'm being called a junkie, so now your sons are too, or are they a different kind of junkie? So what do I call you? Oh, I get it now; you're an alcoholic junkie." She got back in the car with her bleak stare and then rolled her eyes.

Chris and I stayed with his sister for a short period of time. One day, Chris and I got into an argument. I moved out of his sister's house and moved in with my aunt. At first, my aunt didn't want him coming over, but then she allowed him to visit. Next thing I knew, he was moving in. I got my job back at Boston Market since Chris and I left on good terms, so we started working together again. This time, I worked in the morning, and he worked in the evenings.

One morning, I went to work, and they did something to the register; they knew I was stealing. Of course, I got fired. Chris quit. I then received a letter saying I was moving into the projects in Garfield Court in Long Branch. I was there for two to three years before I got evicted for non-payment of rent due to my addiction. This was the life I thought was wonderful. Chris and I would get into fights.

Like in Florida, we fought over a fan. I asked him to come into the bedroom so we could share the fan and watch a movie. He told me to get the fuck out of his face. I made myself very clear: I said, "You don't want to share the fan, then I'm going to cut the cord, so then we both will sweat." His response was, "I'm going to punch you in the face." I went into the kitchen, got a knife, and cut the cord. He jumped up and lunged at me. I grabbed the clock and snatched it out of the socket. All I knew was that I kept swinging and swinging, then I ran into the bathroom. He was begging me to come out. I said, "Hell no!" He yelled how hurt he was, and I said, "So!" All of a sudden, it got quiet. One hour went by, two hours went by.

I came out of the bathroom, and he was nowhere to be found. He finally came into the house. I jumped up, and he said, "I'm sorry; I went to the hospital." By the look of things, he couldn't walk. He said when he got to the hospital, the doctors and nurses thought he got jumped by somebody. The hospital was right over the bridge from where we lived. He said he almost passed out; he had knots on his head, and his testicle was badly cut.

I responded, "This wouldn't have happened only if you shared the fan." We had plenty of bad fights. I would wait until he fell asleep and smoke up all the drugs, then I would blame it on the dog. One day he woke up; I guess he realized the drugs weren't in his pocket. I put empty bags next to the dog. That's why I was stealing from my jobs to support this habit, the habit that I couldn't say no to.

Welfare put me up in a motel for 30 days. It was getting close for me to leave; I had been signed up for Section 8. So it was the evening I walked to Subway. I started talking to the lady who was making my subs. I'm telling her that I have less than 10 days to be out of the motel. She asked if I heard about the housing alliance. I said no, what is it? She replied, "Go over there in the morning." They opened up at 8:30 AM. I was there. I told them my story of being homeless and then told them I was on the Section 8 list.

They called the Red Bank Housing Authority. When they hung up, the woman who made the phone call said, "Honey, gather all your paperwork." She told me everything I needed. It was between me and one other woman from New Orleans; they were giving Section 8 out to Hurricane Katrina survivors.

I left and ran around all that day getting whatever paperwork I could find. I called Section 8 the next morning and told them I had all my paperwork. Even though my time had run out from being in the hotel, my friend allowed us to stay with her. Her name was Deb; we've been friends since 8th grade. She also allowed my kids to stay with her when they came back from Florida.

I made an appointment to see my therapist. I shared stories with her, and after each session, she would ask how I felt. I explained that I felt better because I was able to share my stories without everyone having a biased opinion. I didn't want people to say, "Oh, it's okay," or "You'll get through it." Evidently, I didn't; I dragged myself down, beating myself up. I asked myself many times, "Do you want to get better or die like this?"

I realized that my therapist had me on drugs. I stopped taking them. How will I ever get better by substituting? I couldn't even keep my eyes open.

It finally took me to go through all these stages of rehab and the halfway house to figure it out. What's your miracle? My miracle is not to pick up the first drug. That's another day I stay alive—not just dying, but dying spiritually. It was a terrible tragedy when I heard about Whitney and her daughter. I wouldn't wish that on anyone, but don't you think for a second that it couldn't happen to you? It could've been me or you. NO! We think we're invisible; it can't happen... NOT me.

Think twice every time you get high. Think about it: could this be my last days here on earth? We never know. On July 3rd, 2018, I celebrated one year of clean time—abstinence from all mind-altering drugs. I'm proud to say that 14 months ago, I was in chains, drowning myself—lost, confused, frustrated, and annoyed, beating myself up. Then I realized I'm not alone; it's nothing to be ashamed of. There are millions of people in the world just like me. There is a solution to every problem. Some people are afraid to ask for help because of the shame and guilt that keeps them getting high.

Then you have people who degrade, beat, and talk about you if you relapse. Just don't be afraid to ask for help. It doesn't matter what other people say; this is your life. If you fall, get back up and try again. Remember riding a bike for the first time? You fall, but we learn to get back up and try again. Eventually, one day, that day we don't fall; we keep riding that bike. After that, we get on our bike and ride and never fall.

I'm on probation for two years. Looking back from then to now, I appreciate it. I could be dead or maybe in prison. At first, I said, "When am I going to stop getting supervised from rehab to the halfway house to jail?" I was told what to do, when to go to bed, when to eat, and when to shower. Now I have to meet with my damn probation officer every two weeks.

But I was determined to have a drink eventually, though at some point, I didn't know when. I was still sick with my stinking thinking. It goes beyond that; IT'S STILL A DRUG! You can't beat the street, for sure; the street will beat you. And when you're gone, the streets are going to still be there, waiting for another victim. You have to want to change.

I thought changing was hard, but it doesn't hurt to change. Changing my mindset and wanting better for myself, knowing in my heart that I can do better—to be a better mother, friend, grandmother, and a better me—has been essential. I appreciate the rehab and halfway house; they made me understand the concept of living a better life. I hated the rehab and the halfway house; I wasn't ready to surrender my behaviors and my addiction. If I hadn't gone to the rehab or the halfway house, I wouldn't have met the ladies of the ISP.

I wake up every morning thanking God. He placed me exactly where I needed to be, and that is when I opened my eyes to reality. I still have fears, but my fear now is not to give up on myself. I can be great, and I need to be still and let God continue to work on me. The things that have happened to me in my life, I'm going to use to make me stronger. I'm no longer going to hurt myself because of the choices that everyone in my life makes. I'm no longer a prisoner, and I'm not going to allow anyone else to take me hostage.

Being on probation just allowed me to meet another person who believed in me. I no longer have to be a victim of drug dependency so I can start my day. It feels so good to wake up every morning, thank God for another day, shower, brush my teeth, and look at myself in the mirror, loving what I'm looking at... and that is me. It feels good to have money in my pocket or to get an honest paycheck and deposit it into a bank account.

It's been a struggle; I was ready to give up, but God showed me not to. In the events of my struggles, I'm not proud of what I did, but I have no regrets. I have no regrets because my entire life has been an experience for me. I'm not rich and don't have much, but I have my calling, and my calling is to stay sober just for today. I'm richer than a rich person (smiling).

I still, to this day, have the letter that I wrote to God. I use that letter so I don't forget where I came from. I remember being at the lowest point in my life, selling my body, experiencing miscarriages and abortions. I was miserable and unhappy. After completing two years of probation, I finally felt free. After handling all my legal obligations, fines, and restitution, I was able to buy a car. The first SUV I had, I worked so hard for; my two oldest grandsons stole it and crashed it. I had no vehicle.

When I did have it, I would go visit my mother, taking her out for her birthday and buying her things for Christmas. I found it in my heart to love her for who she was—my mother who gave birth to me. As for my brothers, we talk on the phone. I hope that someday they can come out of prison to live a healthy life.

I said in the beginning that I never stole, but I did. After going through points in my life, I did steal from people. The reflection of my behaviors led me to be a better person today because God had a different plan for me. He had mercy over my life and created the path that I'm supposed to live. I'm happy for it. I'm still involved with the ladies of ISP; I became a witness and then the ambassador of hope. God placed these ladies in my life for a purpose.

I cater when I can, and I have a state job. With my record, I never thought that I would ever get a job like this. DON'T EVER UNDERESTIMATE THE POWER OF GOD! God is now my rock; He has shown me the miracle of His work. Coming Out of the Woods is when I found God again, and I also found me. I'm enjoying the small things in life. I see clearly now; no more rock, tree, nor woods can block my vision or my thoughts.

People who are facing addiction or mental illness, you're never alone. Now I can sleep well at night; I don't need drugs or medication. Everyone does things differently and prays differently, so whomever the God of your understanding is, seek Him/Her/It—anything that will help you. I PRAY FOR GUIDANCE, UNDERSTANDING, STRENGTH, and WISDOM. This is how I can wake up each morning, just knowing that God is there watching over me, that He's in my presence.

There's not a day that goes by when I'm not thanking, praising, and glorifying His name. I'M NO LONGER ALONE OR FEEL ALONE. Chris passed away from renal failure in 2023. We were the best of friends. Sometimes it's better being friends. I would drive down to Long Branch, and we would go for a ride or out to lunch and chat and laugh. Never did we talk about the past; we just enjoyed the moment.

Rest in peace, Chris!

TEARS of the HEART

She taught me everything I know today. Everything was wrong. When I tried to do things right, it was wrong. I started to believe that everything about me was WRONG! It was easy to always go back to being and doing wrong; I was comfortable with wrong growing up. We don't pay attention to the small things in life. Once we get older and have our own children, we learn to teach them what we've learned along the way—and it was wrong!

All the anger that I felt has subsided. She could no longer tell me why or how she died in my heart a long time ago. It was so hard to forget, but in my heart, I knew I had to forgive.

REMEMBERING THE DAY I CAME TO YOU AND ASKED WHY?! Why did you allow my father's friends to molest me and my own cousin to rape me? The only thing you could say to me was, "He was your dad's friend, and he said he didn't do it." BUT! You carried me in your body for nine months. You didn't care enough about me. I guess you didn't; you treated me like shit since I could remember. I came to my mother, that very woman that pushed me out, but you didn't believe me, that very child you held in your arms, BUT you didn't care enough. I was your daughter, your child, BUT I guess you didn't care enough.

The day had come! I didn't expect it at all. I just visited her a month prior. She asked me to make her a doctor's appointment. After getting the date and time, I told her I would come down the night before to stay the night so I could take her. She seemed fine. I came home from work, and as I sat on the sofa to relax, sipping on a glass of wine before showering, my phone rang. It was my daughter, Lateria, crying hysterically. She said, "Mommy's dead." I said, "Wait, WHAT? DEAD!" I asked how she knew. She replied that the police called her and proceeded to give me the number to the police and the medical examiner's office. I stood stiff in disbelief! I said, "Oh GOD, she died alone." My head was spinning. My girlfriend, CT, came out of the bathroom. I looked in her face sadly, and she looked in my face and knew something was wrong. I said, "My mother is gone, she's dead." As she consoled me, I just couldn't accept that she was gone. I didn't know what to say or think.

When my mother passed, she was living in Asbury Park, N.J. I lived in East Orange, N.J. Now I'm thinking, how am I going to get to Asbury Park? My daughter, Tiarrah, called me and said, "Did you hear?" I replied, "Yes!" She then said she was on her way to pick me up. That was a relief. All the way to Monmouth County, I didn't know whether to go to Long Branch or to my mom's apartment in Asbury Park. I called the medical examiner's office and asked if they had my mother there. I gave them her name, and they put me on hold. It seemed like it was forever for them to return to the phone. When the examiner came back on the phone, she said, "Yes, we have your mother." I felt numb; I felt like a piece of me died with her that day. I responded, "Can I come there?" Her reply was, "No, due to COVID, no one can come to the office anymore."

We were riding down the parkway, and the ride seemed so long as we approached Long Branch to see my aunt, my mother's sister, to ask her what to do. I've never had to plan a funeral. I went to ask for guidance. Help! I told her I thought my mother had little to no life insurance to start processing anything. I didn't have money to get her from the morgue. She said she couldn't help me. I didn't come to ask for money.

I left her house to go to the Asbury Police Department because now I needed to get inside my mother's apartment. The officer I knew accompanied me to make sure I got into her apartment to get whatever documents I needed. I figured I would stay the night in her apartment so I could handle things. I went in, but the odor was so bad I couldn't stay there. The sofa where she passed away had defecation on it. I opened up all the windows; it was July, so it was hot. I grabbed whatever I could, and the maintenance of the building locked the door behind me.

I'm thinking, my God! I just spoke with her three days ago. She seemed fine; we talked and laughed over the phone. When we spoke, I asked her if she was updated on her life insurance because the last time I visited her, I told her the policy she had was no good. She assured me that she took care of everything. She was so adamant about having life insurance that there was no doubt in my mind she wouldn't have a policy. I also told my mom not to put this burden on me; I had no money.

I felt like this was another slap in the face. Again, you left me in the dark, scared and alone. Now I don't know what to do. You're gone! Oh Mama, where do I go from here? You taught me to be strong, but I'm weak with no strength to fight. I said, "I know God isn't a myth; He is my gift." I raised my head to the heavens. "I know you are with me; please guide me. My heart is crying, full of hurt and tears."

I went over to my cousin Bobby's house. His girlfriend, Melanie, was trying to help me sort out how to process all this in my mind, but I couldn't process any of it. The one person I knew that wouldn't have hesitated to help me was my aunt, my mother's other sister, but she was in the hospital. Nobody expected her to live due to COVID-19. Melanie started having me call funeral homes; they all were talking about thousands of dollars. I said, "I don't have thousands of dollars."

The next thing for me to do was start a GoFundMe page. I was so embarrassed. I was asking people for money to bury my mom, and I felt so humiliated. Cousin Bobby was furious, yelling at me to go to family. Family said they couldn't help me. With tears coming down my face, I left Bobby's house around 1-2 AM, driving back to Elmwood Park. My daughter Lateria let me use her car to get around.

I went back to work. At work, my mind was all over the place. I had no choice but to go back to work. I was thinking, I don't have money, so I was going to leave her at the morgue. I was left with decisions and choices, and I had no clue how I was going to solve the situation.

I'm not thinking of anger; I'm thinking, is this what life has dealt me? I'm thinking about how my children hated me because I wasn't the parent they needed me to be. When I couldn't, I didn't know how. I apologized so many times. Will there ever be a time when forgiveness sets in so everyone can live their lives? I admit I was wrong. I had scrapes and bruises that I haven't recovered from, but I've always learned to get back up, dust myself off, and keep going. I'm still learning today, even in my darkest days when the skies are gray.

As tears fell from my eyes, in my life, I was a nobody. You taught me through your anger and bitterness. I went through it, not knowing what direction to take, yet I was lost and lonely. You had no dreams for me, and I had none either. I was trying to be somebody, but I was still a nobody. I even grew up believing that!

I ask myself, how can I get through this day? I got the strength and started to reach out to people. Some people gave money towards my mother. All the people my mother helped—I would've thought those people would've come forward. I decided I didn't need friends, but I had to start somewhere. My cousin Regina reached out to me and said to call Aunt Margaret. I didn't know what to expect; I was nervous. I said, "God, why should I call? Just for them to tell me they can't help me? I already know that!" I couldn't take another letdown or another slap in the face.

When I decided to call, we talked! We set up a family meeting at Aunt Pauline's house. The meeting went on for three weeks. In the meantime, I went to my mother's apartment and started cleaning it out. I would like to thank my nephews, Qualek and Jaki Dotts, my daughter Tiarrah, and Rayquan and Clarice Thompson. It took us two to three days to clean.

The money I found in my mother's apartment I was able to use to rent the hall for the repast. By now, I knew family wanted to help. The meeting at Aunt Pauline's house turned out to be fun. We talked about memories when they had black and white pictures. Aunt Pauline showed us a picture when she was a dish—she was young and skinny and had a nice shape. She cooked collard greens, shrimp, mac & cheese, and fish. We sat at the table, eating and talking about the good ol' days. It was Regina, Tasha, both my daughters Tiarrah and Lateria, and Aunt Margaret. Aunt Margaret brought a bag of shoes, and we all were trying them on to see who could fit her shoes. Aunt Margaret had name-brand shoes that looked new.

By the end of the meeting, they were asking me about what I thought or what I liked. I still couldn't wrap my mind around it all. Mom was dead, and I was planning her funeral. I really wasn't ready. I was thinking my brothers are in prison; they're never going to see her again. I didn't have the money to bring them home to see her for the last time. We decided on having her cremated. We called Lawson Funeral Home in Long Branch, N.J. He said he would take care of everything. He went to get my mother from the morgue. The next day, we were able to go see her for the last time. I couldn't cry; I just stared.

Afterward, we all departed and went back home, trying to set a date for her memorial. Storming, thundering, and lightning; rain was pouring. I felt like I needed to go outside. I didn't know whether I wanted to cry or scream. I told CT I wanted to go outside. She replied, "Outside in the storm?" I said, "Yes, outside in the storm." She said, "Okay, outside we go." We got our rain boots and jackets out of the closet and grabbed the umbrella by the door. She said, "Wait! Wait! Why are we going outside?" I said, "I want to cry; I can hide the tears in the rain." She said, "You don't have to go outside to hide your tears. I have a shoulder, and my arms are open. I'm here for you." I said, "Yeah, I know. I want to go outside in the rain." So we both went outside, tears falling from my eyes as we walked around the apartment complex.

She said something silly and funny, as she always does, and I started to laugh. Then we began stomping and splashing in the flooded waters. Our feet were soaked and wet, but I felt better. When we got back in the house, she said, "Do you want a bubble bath?" I said, "That sounds good." She lit three candles and put on soothing music—light jazz—as I laid back to rest my head on the back of the bathtub. Thoughts were going through my mind: this pain, these tears that are falling from my eyes won't last forever. Tears of the heart last always. I took a deep breath and sighed. I closed my eyes, enjoying the smell of the candles;

it was comforting. I didn't think about anything. I cleared my head and embraced the moment, then relaxed.

I know now how to walk with my head held high, gracefully and with gratefulness. There are a lot of rainy days, but on the other side of things, rainy days make things grow. Mom, you gave me the strength to live. Before you passed on, I'm glad I was able to speak to you and tell you how I forgave you when we last spoke over the phone.

We never know why we do the things we do to hurt others. Like the time when I took your brother to court for seducing my child, and you thought it was okay for him to do that. You were my mother and my child's grandmother, and you stood in court on his side. That hurt me to my heart. Was I surprised? No, not really. I've even asked other family members if you were raped or touched as kids. Everyone said no, including you.

We have to be held accountable for our actions; they will come back to haunt us one way or another. Kids remember; they know; they have feelings too. How could you look that kid in the face that you raped, molested, or even mistreated? Twenty years later, they will remember the person that did those horrible things to them. They will remember you. Twenty years of pain, guilt, stripped of their innocence, stripped of their childhood. People will always remember what you stole from them!

I've always felt safe around all my uncles. I remember my mother's brothers would come get me some weekends. At the time, my mother had five brothers; four used to come get us on the weekends. I say "us" because it was my cousins too. When this uncle tried to seduce my daughter, I called the other cousins from my mother and asked if he had ever raped or touched them. They all said no, and I said me either. I was angry because I never expected him, nor any of my uncles on my mother's side, to be like this. When she told me, I was lost for words; I couldn't believe it. I asked if she was sure, and she said, "Mom, yes."

See, when I was raped and molested, I taught my kids to be outspoken. I always told them I would protect them against predators. He did it because my brothers said she was "fresh" and "you're her uncle." The things my brothers did to her, I believe that's why they're suffering. My daughter is doing wonderfully, but people from our family started degrading her. She was 16 and pregnant. I don't know what gave people the right to think it was okay, calling me on the phone and saying hateful things. All he could say was, "I was getting high." What the hell did that have to do with it? You can never trust family!

But I forgave them all so I can move on with my life.

The visit of forgiveness.

I haven't been to my father's grave since he passed away. I didn't even go to his funeral or burial. I had to call to find out where he was buried. I decided to go visit his grave. He was a veteran, so I just one day woke up and went. I really didn't know what I was going to say. As I was driving, the ride was an hour and a half. It was a good drive; it was a nice, sunny, hot day.

This is what I said to my father:

"Dad, now I know! I know now because I lived it. You weren't a bad father; your decisions and choices were. But I see we were not all perfect people. Not all my life was bad; I remember the good times too. The difference between you and me is that I just didn't stand by and let my children be raped or molested. I know I was a handful, and even though I was bad, I still didn't deserve it. It will forever be with me, but I will not let it destroy my spirit again. If there was any harm I brought to my children, I caused it by being an addict and not being there, just like you weren't there. And God gave me chances to get it right. You're in the grave; I'm not. I have a chance to get it right this time.

Father, I forgive you, and I truly love you! I claimed my victory over my life. I'm doing great now. I thought you should know I graduated high school in 2010. Even though my brothers are in prison, we talk. Hopefully, they both can come out here and do right. It's time to break these chains and come out of the woods of addiction. There was a lot of damage done. Not only did you leave us, but you also left three other kids and grandkids. Even your other children you had are all screwed up, but they're doing well except for little James.

I had a chance to share 16 years of memories with you, and my brothers were 8 when you left. Your other kids didn't get a chance to know you; they just want to know where they came from. They ask a lot of questions, and I can only share my experiences that I had with you."

I got back into my car. As I was exiting the cemetery, a mile up the road, it started pouring rain. It was raining so hard that I had to pull over. I called my daughter Tiarrah, and we talked for a moment. Once the rain slowed down, we hung up. I continued to drive, and the sun came back out. As I got on the parkway, I drove a mile or two, doing 80-90 mph. I ran into the pouring rain, trying to slow down; I couldn't even see the car in front of me. I quickly put my hazards on.

There, I said to myself, my father must've been happy that I came to visit. Now it was just tears of joy.

THE LETTER

(Listen to "The Battle Is the Lord's" by Yolanda Adams)

When I first met you, you were white as snow. When no one was there for me, you were. You made me feel safe; you never talked about me, judged me, nor used me. You solved every problem, whether whatever I was going through or upset. You comforted me. Our uniqueness and friendship made us different from others. You made me need you more and more; I also started to depend on you. I couldn't focus on anything but you. I sold my body and soul just to have you. I ended up in jail because of you. I ended up in institutions because of you. I laid awake every night thinking about you, wishing you were here, mourning for you to come back to me.

You were my disease! You kept me from my family. I neglected my kids because I loved you more. I lost and got evicted because I loved you more. I thought you loved me! In the end, I realized you were harmful. You kept me in the darkness of isolation; you destroyed my life because I allowed you to!

I now have to say goodbye. We can no longer be friends. I feel better without you! I moved on to a better life, the life that has been waiting for me. Now I see the light; I can now look at myself in the mirror and love ME. My God! My trophy, rescue me from the bottomless pits of you! You're no longer my battle to fight.

Goodbye, cocaine!

(Listen to "I Got Joy" by CeCe Winans)

(Listen to "A Great Day to Be Alive" by Travis Tritt)

Rest in peace to those who passed away due to addiction! My heart and condolences go out to the families. Addiction can enter every family; it comes into your family to seek and destroy lives. Addiction also takes and steals lives. I've witnessed it, saw it, and I also lived it. It makes you do things you normally wouldn't do: selling your body, stealing, and/or killing or being killed. The families are the ones who suffer the most, not being able to save you or do anything about it until you get help.

It's true what they say: jail, institutions, and death—that's true. I thought every time that I was determined to prove that I could beat the street. I chose to live and not to die trying to prove a point. I surrendered; I couldn't win. I do have children and grandchildren who love me; I just had to love myself.

www.ingramcontent.com/pod-product-compliance
Lightning Source LLC
Chambersburg PA
CBHW061259130225
21884CB00022B/1708